Ruff Smells Hot Dogs

By Carmel Reilly

Will and Jill went for a run with Ruff.

"Ruff can smell the buds!" said Will.

'It's not the buds
Ruff can smell," said Jill.

Ruff ran up the hill.

Sniff, sniff!

"Ruff! Here, Ruff," yells Will.

But Ruff ran on.

Will and Jill ran up the hill.

"Ruff is at the well," said Jill.

"No," said Will.

"Ruff is not at the well.

Ruff is at the grill!"

"Ruff can smell the grill!"
said Jill.

"He will get the hot dogs,"
yells Will.
"It will be a mess!"

Sniff, sniff!

Will and Jill ran.

The man got a hot dog off the grill.

Ruff sat up.

The hot dog fell.

A gull got it!

"Yap, yap, yap!" said Ruff.

CHECKING FOR MEANING

1. What did Will think Ruff could smell? *(Literal)*

2. What did Ruff do when the man got a hot dog off the grill? *(Literal)*

3. Why didn't Ruff stop when Will called him? *(Inferential)*

EXTENDING VOCABULARY

yells	How do you speak if you *yell*? Is this a loud sound or a soft sound? What other words describe how people speak loudly? E.g. shout, call, scream, bellow, roar.
well	What is the purpose of the *well* in the story? What are other meanings of this word? Can you use it in a sentence to show a different meaning?
grill	What is a *grill*? What is another name for a grill? E.g. barbecue. What can you cook on a grill?

MOVING BEYOND THE TEXT

1. Have you had a meal cooked on a grill? Did you enjoy the food?

2. What do you need to do to be safe near a grill?

3. Why was Ruff able to smell the hot dogs, but the children couldn't?

4. What jobs do dogs do in our community because they have a good sense of smell?

SPEED SOUNDS

ff	ll	ss	zz

PRACTICE WORDS

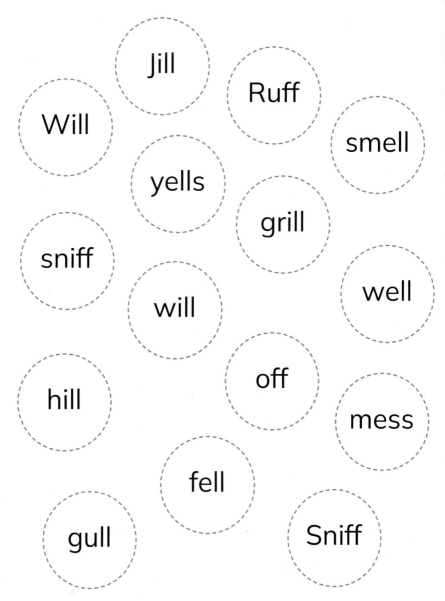

Jill

Ruff

Will

smell

yells

grill

sniff

will

well

hill

off

mess

fell

gull

Sniff